D0537322

Donna Kooler's Cross Stitch
Inspirations

Bookspan
Garden City, New York

ISBN 0-7394-3900-6
Printed in the U.S.A.

Table of Contents

	Photo	Chart

Perched on a hill in the suburbs of San Francisco sits the charming city of Pleasant Hill, California. Few people would guess that this rather prosaic office building harbors a magical world: the home of the Kooler Design Studio, Inc. The Studio is one of America's top design companies, and behind it all is Donna Kooler, the studio's president and co-founder.

This unusual company has its roots in Donna's work as Design Director for *Sunset Designs*, the premier needlework company in the 70's and early 80's. Donna graduated from art school in Los Angeles in the 1950's, and while raising her children, she found great pleasure in the art of needlepoint. While her art training enabled her to begin designing and stitching her own needlepoint—it didn't take long for Donna to translate that personal pleasure into a full time job. She directed the creativity of *Sunset Designs* until the company was sold in 1985 and was moved to Georgia.

By that time Donna had gathered around her a group of talented artists and stitchers who not only loved needlework, but also had great ideas and an uncanny feel for what the consumer wanted. In 1985 Donna, together with her Sunset staff of designers, founded Kooler Design Studio Inc.

Donna decided early on to license the work to publishers and kit manufacturers. This allowed the studio to concentrate on what they do best: **create and design**. Today their work appears world wide in books, kits, CD's and magazines. The studio is proud to be associated with the world's leading publishers and manufacturers: *American School of Needlework, Leisure Arts, Sterling Publishing, Origin Publishing, Janlynn, Bucilla, PatternMaker by Hobbyware* and *Dimensions*.

Donna Kooler

The studio is located in one of the most beautiful places in the country. The area supports every kind of natural beauty from sunny beaches to beckoning mountains. On their way to work, the employees at the Kooler Studio can see Mt. Diablo dressed for the changing seasons sometimes hiding in the fog or gleaming in the sunlight or displaying its snowcapped peaks. The studio, no less wonderful, is filled with dolls, bears, bunnies, antique toys, folk art, quilts and paintings. Needlework and thread abound everywhere. Stitched samples of finished pieces and works in progress are on the walls; books line shelves, and neat rows of thread populate many of the rooms. The staff can be found creating in every nook and cranny of the crowded studio.

Walk into the offices and suddenly the season seems out of kilter. On a humid summer day, the desks and walls are covered with an astonishment of snowflakes and everything is in red and green. In winter "quite the other way" sunlit fields and pastures dominate the studio desks and walls. The demands of the business world necessitate their working at least six months in advance of the season, and the Kooler designers do not think this strange.

Designs usually begin as drawings and are then turned into projects by the Studio's team of highly-qualified stitchers, who are actually assistant designers. They chart, adapt, translate, interpret and stitch the designs before they are published. The stitchers and designers work together to perfect the design, such as looking for colors that might be too close. Each assistant designer brings additional talents to her job. One might enjoy doing crewel, another ribbon embroidery, a third quilting. This allows the studio to be versatile and create designs for many forms of needlework and crafts.

The group has worked together in one capacity or another for almost thirty years and together they produce over 100 kits, 40 leaflets and five or six hardcover books each year. In addition to needlework books, the team also produces books on decorative painting, glass painting, crocheting, knitting, and scrapbooking—even a series of books on planning weddings.

Every design that leaves the Kooler Studio bears Donna's imprint. Nothing is produced without her final approval or guidance. The samplers in this collection of inspirational cross-stitch, while not created by her, reflect much of Donna's personal philosophy.

Linda Gillum is co-founder of Kooler Design Studio and is its executive vice president. Linda, an award winning designer, is one of the top Kooler Studio designers. A fine artist and an enormously diverse designer, her talent is expressed in all design disciplines. Linda's artistic background is in watercolors, oil paintings, doll

making and pastel drawings. She has a degree in business from St. Mary's College in Moraga, California and a degree in art from the College of Arts and Crafts in Oakland, California. Many of the works in this collection are from this talented designer.

Linda Gillum

Being a part of a group of creative people who are supportive and inspiring is what Linda enjoys most about her work at the Kooler Studio. There is always something being shared: new ideas, new techniques, new interests. If she is stuck on a design problem, she only has to step out of her office to find people with any number of solutions.

Donna and Linda's relationship is based on mutual respect and admiration—and a very close friendship. They recognize each one's strengths and weaknesses and trust each other to do what is best for the business and each other.

Priscilla Timm, another founding member of the company who serves as a vice president, is the primary project manager for all design projects. Nothing leaves the studio without her final stamp of approval.

The studio's amazing group of award winning designers include Barbara Baatz Hillman, Nancy Rossi, Sandy Orton, Jorja Hernandez, Basha Kooler Hanner and a long list of free-lance designers.

The rest of the staff; editors, writers, proofreaders, and photographers include Judy Swager, Barbara Kuhn, Jessica Main, Kit Schlich, JoLynn Taylor, Nancy Wong, Marsha Hinkson, Sara Angle, Jennifer Drake, Virginia Handley-Rivett, Char Randolph, Karen, Linnea Wiser, Joellen Angel and Dianne Woods.

Last by not least is Oscar, the studio's mixed-breed mascot, who for the past eleven years has entertained everyone with his personality. He gathers pats, praises and treats while keeping everyone fit with his frequent requests for walks. He can be seen photographed in many of the Kooler designed books.

Excellence has always been the standard of the Kooler Design Studio, whether they are working with silk threads on fine linen, painting on wood, appliquéing on fabric or stitching with acrylic yarn on plastic canvas. They believe in the quality of their designs as well as the thoroughness of the development of each project.

"As a group," says Donna, "our mission is to provide quality products to our customers who take pleasure and pride in stitching and displaying our designs in their homes. We are committed to this goal." It is the quality of the designs as well as the thoroughness the Studio takes in development them that makes the Kooler Design Studio so successful. Look for the Kooler Design Studio, Inc. logo on books, kits and CD's in your local book and craft store or online at www.koolerdesign.com.

Kooler Design Studio

God is Our Hope

designed by Linda Gillum

In good times and in hard times,
hope gives us the strength and
will to go on. The story of the
Crucifixion (and the Resurrection)
reminds us never to take leave
of hope, which is meat and
drink to our souls.

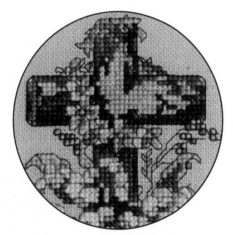

chart on page 62

9

Sustain Me
with Raisins

designed by Donna Vermillion Giampa

What is love?
The Song of Solomon
beautifully described true
love with these words:
"Sustain me with raisins, refresh
me with apples, as I am faint with
love." {*Song of Songs, 2:3*}
Indeed love can be all-consuming,
whether love of family, friend or
faith. To know love and to be
loved are precious gifts.

chart on page 64

May the Work of My Hand

designed by Holly De Font

Our faith leads us to create in
whatever way we choose,
whether we plow the field,
hammer the nail, sing the song
or paint the masterpiece.
Whatever we do, if we do it
well and with good heart,
we can be sure it will be
a welcome gift to the world.

chart on page 66

God Gave us Music

designed by Linda Gillum

God gave us music so that we
could pray without words,
with the sound of our joy, each
in our own way.
Music is a special gift to
those who cannot see.
And yet to hear, we must
remember to listen.

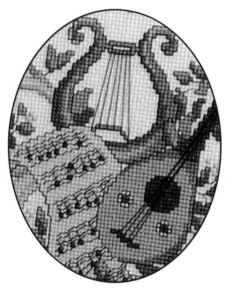

chart on page 68

The Voice of the Turtle

designed by Donna Vermillion Giampa

Turtles do not have a voice, or at
least not one we can hear. When
in Song of Songs, Solomon wrote
"…the flowers appear on the
earth, the time of singing is come,
and the voice of the turtle is heard
throughout the land…" he was
referring to the turtledove, the
bird whose gentle song heralds
the arrival of each new spring,
and with it, renewal.

Flowers appear on the earth; the time of the singing of birds is come, and the voice of the turtle is heard in our land.
Song of Solomon 2:12

Thank You, Lord

designed by Holly De Font

This cry of thanks leaps to our lips
many times each day, as we walk
through the places and hours that
make up our lives. Each of us has
a special reason to give thanks,
although we may not always
know what the reason is.

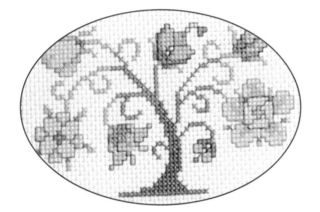

chart on page 72

To Those Who Believe. . .

designed by Linda Gillum

Angels are special beings, not man, not deity,
but ephemeral forces who watch over and
sometimes guide us. Are they real? No one
really knows, but we honor them when we
say of a favorite person, "She's an angel."
Remember to thank the angels in your life.

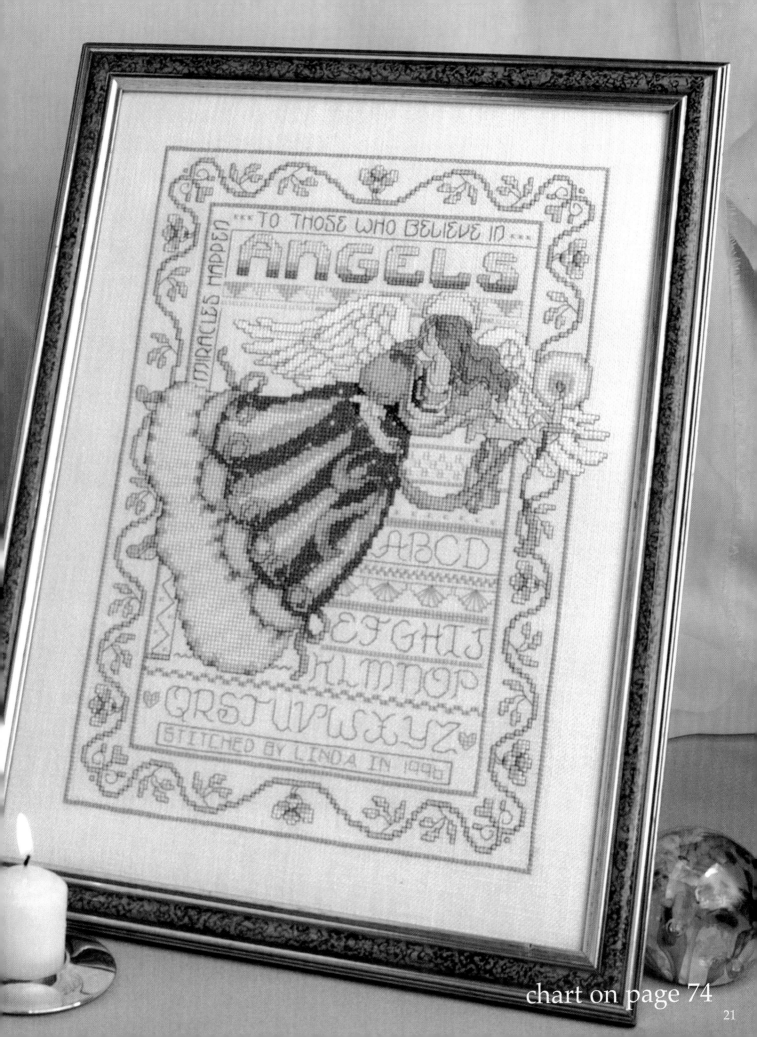

chart on page 74

All Creatures Praise the Lord

designed by Linda Gillum

All creatures paise the Lord, and live each lovely
day without thought or plan for the future.
The rainbow symbolizes the radiant beauty of our
world that is enjoyed and honored by all creatures
on the earth. Whether they have two feet or four,
slither on the ground or soar in the sky, all creatures
stand in awe of what has been created.

chart on page 78

23

Water My Garden

designed by Linda Gillum

No matter how carefully a seed is planted, without water it will not grow. From birth to old age, all of us must be sustained by the support of those who care. A neglected garden needs frequent attention to reach its full potential, as do we all.

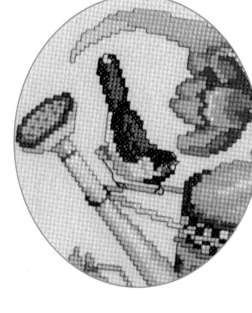

... WATER MY GARDEN
AND
DRENCH MY FLOWER BEDS
Ecclesiasticus 24 x 31

chart on page 80

A Day Hemmed in Prayer

designed by Holly De Font

Each dream we have, each action we take, each word we say, is woven into the fabric of our lives forever. If we neatly hem each day with prayer, our fabric will be beautiful and will live forever.

A DAY HEMMED IN
PRAYER IS
SELDOM UNRAVELS

chart on page 83

27

Lilies on the Cross

designed by Linda Gillum

The beauty and sweet scent of pure white lilies remain always in our memories as we reflect on the meaning of the Resurrection. "For God so loved the world…" is one of the first things we teach our children about the Christian religion.

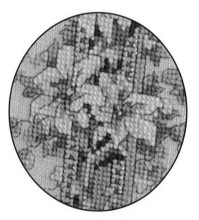

chart on page 84

Bless Thy Beasts and Singing Birds

designed by Linda Gillum

Bless thy beasts and singing birds for
these are among the greatest treasures
of our world. We teach our children to
appreciate, respect and to treat kindly
all that the Lord has created.

chart on page 86

Consider the Lilies

designed by Donna Vermillion Giampa

One of the most beloved Bible passages
is in Matthew which tells us to
"Consider the lilies and how they grow…"
which demonstrates the power of faith
to provide that which we need.
A plant struggles its way up through
a crack in the concrete sidewalk,
believing it will find the sun and water
it needs to flower.

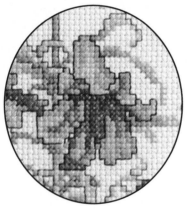

chart on page 88

Whoever Eats My Bread

designed by Holly De Font

When we break the loaf together, we often share our hopes, our dreams and our beliefs. Indeed we may even sing the same song, in harmony with each other and with the earth.

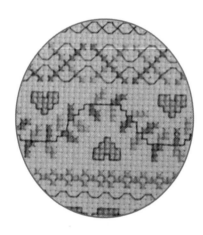

chart on page 90

Believe

designed by Linda Gillum

To believe is to exist; when we go
to bed, we believe we will see the
new dawn; when we leave our
home, we believe we will return.
We believe the spring will come,
the snow will fall. We believe in
the moon and the stars, though
we have no proof of any of these
beliefs. And so we believe in God
and His angels, not proven,
but not doubted.

chart on page 92

37

Give Thanks to God

designed by Linda Gillum

Thank you, God, for our blue sky,
For fish that swim, for mountains high.

For butterflies and teddy bears,
For teaching me to say my prayers.

Thank you, God, for birds' strong wings,
Thank you God for everything.

chart on page 94

Land of Oil-Olive and Honey

designed by Donna Vermillion Giampa

To ancient people, important staples
included olive oil and sweet honey, almost
enough in themselves to sustain life.
Thus to them, the land of oil and honey
was the Holy Land, where they would
find all that was necessary for life.

chart on page 98

Each Day is a New Beginning

designed by Linda Gillum

What was, was; what will be, will be; what is, is today. Each dawn brings us a bright new beginning. Each new day, we can put away the sorrows, worries and regrets of the past, and concentrate on making the most of the day that is here. Let us enjoy each precious hour for its own sake.

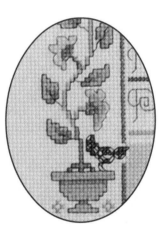

chart on page 100

Welcome Angels

designed by Sandy Orton

Who would not welcome an angel into his life? Angels give us something to strive for, something to dream about, and something to calm our being and soothe our soul.

chart on page 104

Send Out Fragrance

designed by Donna Vermillion Giampa

It is the sweet scent that attracts
the bee to the flower, the moth to
the cactus bloom. In our daily
lives, we constantly send out
signals to others—come close,
step back, go away. Take care that
the signals you give represent
your true message.

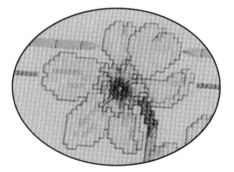

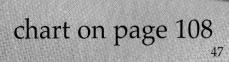

chart on page 108

Consider the Wondrous Works

designed by Holly De Font

At those moments when we are afraid,
sad or in pain, let us think instead on the
wonderful works that surround us, from
a towering tree, a great river, a new-born
baby, to an eagle in flight; these sustain us
and fuel our sense of wonder.

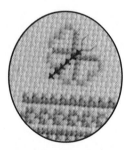

chart on page 110

The Preaching of the Cross

designed by Linda Gillum

The power of God is in the preaching of the cross
which is in many ways exemplified by the roses,
violets and other flowers that enrich our lives.
For the seed is planted, the flower blooms,
drops its seed as widely as it can, then dies.
But the seeds from its heart live on.

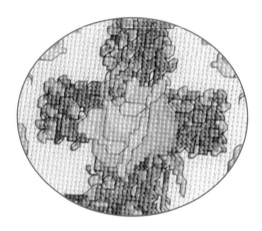

chart on page 112

Music is a Gift from God

designed by Linda Gillum

Music is a special gift from God that
enters the soul of man and lifts our hearts
with feeling. All creatures give praise with
music; in song, in the sound of
voices, in the call of the birds. If we listen,
music is all around us. Not in the loud
numbing beat of the radio, but in the quiet
breeze in the trees, the sound of the ocean
tides, the cry of a baby.

Music is a gift from God

chart on page 114

53

Angels Gather Here

designed by Linda Gillum

Where else but in the sky, flying
free toward the sun and the
moon, would angels gather?
Their beautiful wings carry them
from above down into the hearts
of those who believe.

chart on page 116

55

For Gifts Beyond Counting

designed by Holly De Font

What is a gift? It is something presented freely, willingly and with good grace, not something we demand of others. A gift may be something prettily wrapped with a bow on top, or it may be a gift of a few hours spent together, or it may be the opening of a door for someone else. Even a dog who shyly offers you a bone presents you with his most precious possession.

chart on page 118

Bless Our Home

designed by Linda Gillum

Our homes, our families are the center of our world. Here we learn to respect and honor those we love; to share what we have with others; and to give gladly without thought of any return. Truly, our homes are where are hearts remain even as we walk away.

chart on page 120

Expect a Miracle

designed by Holly De Font

We do not need to believe in
miracles, for every day they will
happen around us anyway.
Many things we expect and
accept are truly miracles,
as much as is the sun which
rises every day, or are the
flaming leaves of autumn.

chart on page

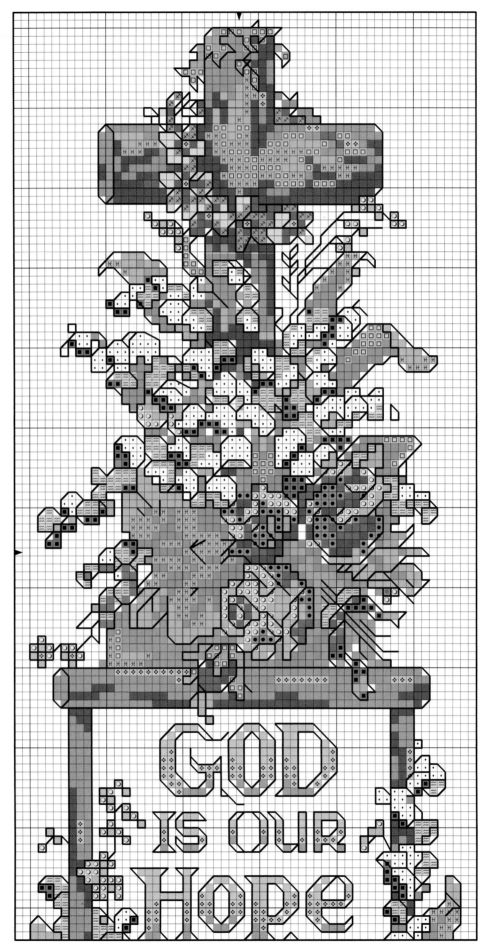

Continue stitching from chart on page 63.

God is Our Hope

Design size: 61 wide x 133 high

Photo model: stitched on a 10" x 15" piece of tea-dyed 28-count linen.

Photo: pages 8 and 9.

		Anchor	DMC
•	= white (flowers)	1	blanc
◦	= lt pink (roses)	36	3326
▨	= dk pink (roses)	38	961
◉	= med red (roses)	46	666
■	= dk red (roses)	47	321
■	= very dk red (roses)	20	815
▥	= yellow-green (leaves)	254	3348
❖	= med green (leaves)	225	702
▩	= dk green (leaves)	246	986
▫	= lt gray-green leaves	214	368
▦	= med gray-green (leaves)	876	3816
∿	= lt turquoise (flowers)	158	747
▥	= med turquoise (flowers)	1038	519
■	= dk turquoise (flowers)	1039	518
	very dk turquoise	162	517
▢	= lt blue (flowers)	128	800
▨	= med blue (flowers)	140	3755
■	= dk blue (flowers)	142	798
▢	= tan (lettering)	361	738
❖	= lt rust		
	(lettering, cross, base)	1047	402
▨	= med rust		
	(lettering, cross, base)	1048	3776
▨	= med brown (cross, base)	355	606
■	= dk brown (cross, base)	359	801
	med gray	400	317
▨	= dk gray (below cross)	236	3799

= Backstitch:

roses, pink buds—very dk red

leaves, stems, moss—dk green

turquoise flowers, bow—very dk turquoise

wood, lettering—dk brown

blue flowers—med gray

Shaded area shows last two rows from chart on page 62.

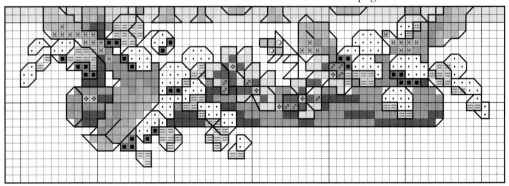

63

Sustain Me
with Raisins

Design size: 80 wide x 141 high

Photo model: stitched on a 12" x 17" piece of antique white 14-count Aida cloth.

Photo: pages 10 and 11.

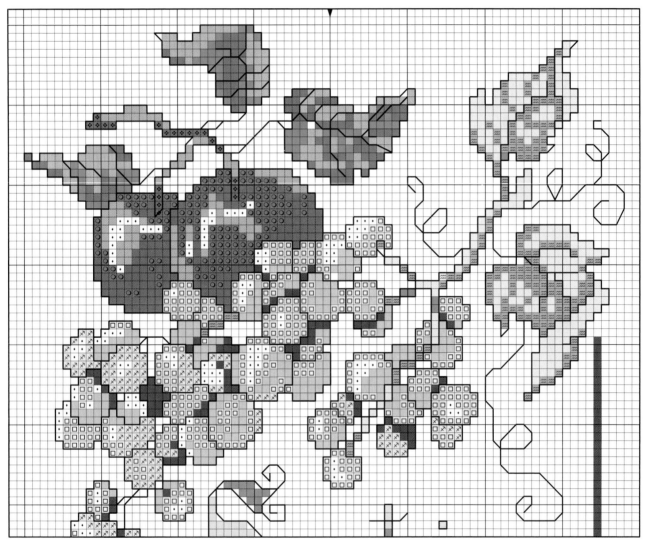

Continue stitching from chart on page 65.

	Anchor	DMC			Anchor	DMC
• = white (apples, yellow grapes)	1	blanc	▩ = med blue (lettering)		1034	931
= cream (apples)	1009	3770	dk blue		1035	930
▦ = lt pink (flowers)	73	963	▨ = lt purple (purple grapes)		109	209
▩ = med pink (flowers)	75	962	▩ = med purple (purple grapes)		110	208
▦ = lt red (apples)	332	946	✳ = tan (apples)		361	738
⊙ = med red (apples)	46	666	▦ = lt brown (stems)		1008	3773
▩ = dk red (apples)	1005	816	▩ = med brown (stems)		1007	3772
◇ = lt yellow (flowers)	301	744	▩ = med dk brown (yellow grapes)		349	301
▢ = med yellow (yellow grapes)	305	743	▪ = dk brown (stems)		310	780
✗ = med dk yellow (yellow grapes)	306	725	gray		400	317
▩ = dk yellow (yellow grapes)	307	783	∣ = Backstitch:			
▩ = lt yellow-green (leaves)	261	989	apples (except center, cut edges & stems)—dk red			
▩ = dk yellow-green (leaves)	262	3363	leaves, stems, tendrils, calyxes—dk green			
▨ = lt green (leaves)	240	966	lettering—dk blue			
▩ = med green (leaves)	226	703	apple stems & branch, zigzag line—med dk brown			
▩ = dk green (leaves)	211	562	yellow grapes, apple centers, cut edges—dk brown			
▨ = lt blue (lettering)	1033	932	flowers, purple grapes—gray			

Shaded area shows last two rows from chart on page 64.

May the Work of My Hand

Design size: 67 wide x 95 high

Photo model: stitched on a 12″ x 14″ piece of antique white 14-count Aida cloth.

Photo: pages 12 and 13.

		Anchor	DMC
· = lt pink (flowers)		74	3354
▦ = dk pink (flowers)		76	961
▦ = gold (zigzag border)		1045	436
▦ = green (outer border)		210	562
○ = lt blue (center border)		121	809
▦ = med blue (lettering)		122	3807
ǀ = Backstitch: med blue			

God Gave us Music

Design size: 86 wide x 155 high

Photo model: stitched on a 12" x 16" piece of white 14-count Aida cloth.

Stitching note: Fill in sheet music with cream.

Photo: pages 14 and 15.

Continue stitching from chart on page 69.

		Anchor	DMC				Anchor	DMC
•	= cream (mandolin)	276	739	▨	= dk rust (mandolin)		351	400
▨	= lt pink (lettering, flowers)	25	3326	▨	= lt brown (harp)		336	758
◉	= med pink (border)	38	961	▢	= med brown (harp)		338	922
	dk pink	39	309	▪	= dk brown (harp)		339	920
	= lt yellow (horn)	301	744	■	= very dk brown (mandolin, notes)		360	898
↗	= med yellow (horn)	305	743	\	= Straight Stitch: very dk brown		
⋙	= dk yellow (horn)	306	725	|	= Backstitch:		
▨	= med gold (horn)	307	783		lettering—dk pink		
	dk gold	308	781		horn outline—dk gold		
	= lt green (leaves)	215	503		leaves, stems, inside borderline—dk green		
▨	= dk green (leaves)	217	561		mandolin—dk rust		
▨	= lt rust (mandolin)	347	402		harp, staff, notes—very dk brown		
⊡	= med rust (mandolin)	349	3776				

Shaded area shows last two rows from chart on page 68.

...Flowers appear on the e
the time of the
singing of birds is o
voice
and
the of the
turtle
is
heard
in our
land
2:12

Continue stitching from chart on page 71.

The Voice of the Turtle

Design size: 114 wide x 115 high

Photo model: stitched on a 14" x 14" piece of antique white 14-count Aida cloth.

Stitching note: If desired, French Knot highlights may be added to the three center birds eyes (white), and turtle eye (very lt brown).

Photo: pages 16 and 17.

		Anchor	DMC
·	= white (birds, flowers)	1	1001
o	= very lt pink (flowers)	271	819
●	= lt pink (flowers)	73	963
	= med pink (flowers)	75	962
	= dk pink (flowers, lettering)	77	3687
	= lt orange (flowers)	313	742
	= med orange (flowers)	314	741
	= dk orange (flowers)	316	970
↗	= lt yellow (flowers)	292	3078
	= med yellow (flowers)	295	726
■	= dk yellow (flowers)	298	972
≈	= very lt yellow-green (leaves)	265	3347
	= lt yellow-green (leaves)	266	471
	= med yellow-green (leaves)	267	469
	= dk yellow-green (leaves)	268	937
	= lt blue-green (leaves)	214	368
✿	= med blue-green (leaves)	216	502
	= dk blue-green (leaves)	218	319
✕	= lt turquoise (birds)	167	519
✤	= med turquoise (birds, lettering)	168	3810
	= dk turquoise (birds)	162	517
	= very dk turquoise (birds, lettering)	164	824
	= very lt brown (birds, borders, turtles, leaves)	372	738
✿	= lt brown (birds, turtle)	373	3828
	= med brown (birds, turtle, lettering)	375	869
	= dk brown (turtle)	360	898
⊠	= lt gray (birds, flowers)	397	3024
	= med gray (birds, flowers)	398	415
	= dk gray (birds)	235	414
■	= black (birds)	403	310

• = French Knots:
   periods before "Flowers"—dk pink
   "i" dots, semicolon, comma, period—med yellow-green
   colon—med turquiose

| = Backstitch:
   gray bird eyes—white
   "Flowers," pink flowers—dk pink
   yellow & white flower centers, orange flower outlines—dk orange
   "appear...the," "of the," "of," "is come," "is...land"—med yellow green
   stems, yellow-green leaves—dk yellow-green
   remaining leaves—dk blue-green
   "time"—med turquoise
   "singing," "birds," turquoise areas of birds, reference—dk turquoise
   "and...turtle," remaining yellow flowers, brown areas
         of birds, blue bird beaks—med brown
   turtle—dk brown
   remaining white flowers, gray ares of birds, bird feet—dk gray
   black areas of birds, blue bird eye, gray bird beaks & wings—black

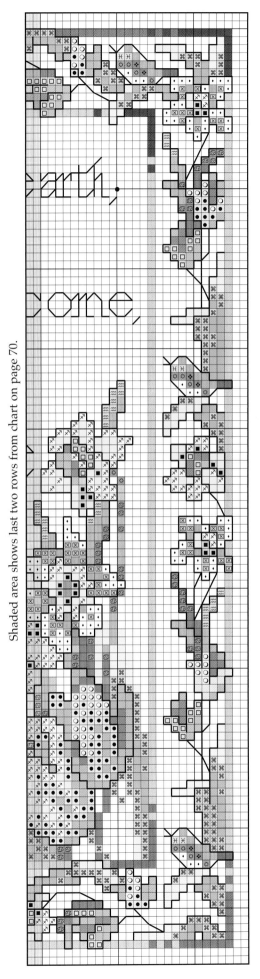

Shaded area shows last two rows from chart on page 70.

Thank You, Lord

Design size: 105 wide x 135 high   Photo: pages 18 and 19.

Photo model: stitched on a 14" x 16" piece of natural 14-count Aida cloth.

Continue stitching from chart on page 73.

Shaded area shows last two rows from chart on page 72.

	Anchor	DMC
• = white (clothing)	1	blanc
= lt pink (clothing, flowers)	24	963
= med pink (clothing, flowers)	31	3708
dk pink	41	956
o = lt peach (people)	778	3774
= dk peach (hat)	35	3801
✳ = lt gold (flower)	361	738
= med gold (flowers, tree)	363	436
= dk gold (flowers, tree)	365	435
= med green (clothing, tenrils, people's tree)	209	913
= dk green (clothing, tendrils, outer border)	211	562
✗ = lt blue (clothing, flowers)	130	809
= med blue (flowers, inner border)	131	798

	Anchor	DMC
= dk blue (words, inner border)	143	797
= lt fuchsia (flowers)	85	3609
= med fuchsia (flowers, inner border)	87	3607
= lt rust (lettering, center border)	1047	402
= med rust (people, lettering, center border)	1048	3776
= brown (people, tree, lettering, center border)	370	434
= gray (rock)	922	930

| = Backstitch:
pink flowers (except gold centers)—dk pink
plant between man and woman—dk green
blue and fuchsia flowers—dk blue
zigzag lines, border lines, cat, dog, hair, gold flowers,
    gold flower centers—brown
remaining outlines—gray

To Those Who Believe...

Design size: 125 wide x 170 high

Photo model: stitched on a 15" x 19" piece of yellow 28-count Meran.

Stitching notes: Use the small upper case alphabet and large numerals on page 124 to work desired message, name, and date with med rust.

Photo: pages 20 and 21.

Continue stitching from chart on page 75.

Continue stitching from chart on page 76.

page 74	page 75
page 76	page 77

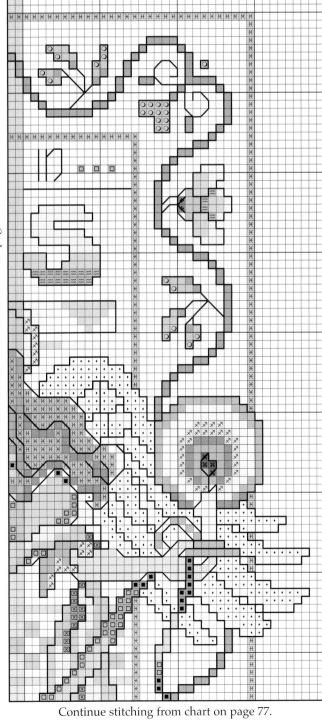

Shaded area shows last two rows from chart on page 74.

Continue stitching from chart on page 77.

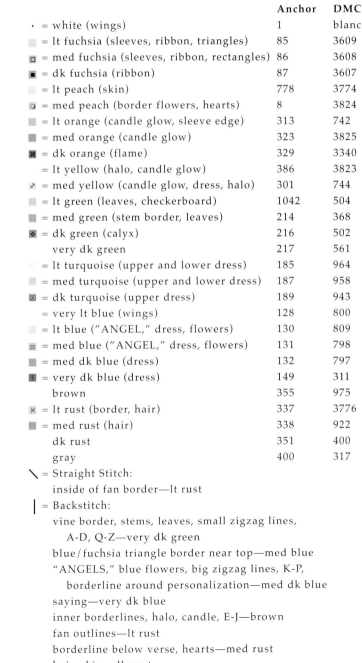

		Anchor	DMC
•	= white (wings)	1	blanc
	= lt fuchsia (sleeves, ribbon, triangles)	85	3609
□	= med fuchsia (sleeves, ribbon, rectangles)	86	3608
■	= dk fuchsia (ribbon)	87	3607
	= lt peach (skin)	778	3774
○	= med peach (border flowers, hearts)	8	3824
	= lt orange (candle glow, sleeve edge)	313	742
	= med orange (candle glow)	323	3825
✦	= dk orange (flame)	329	3340
	= lt yellow (halo, candle glow)	386	3823
↗	= med yellow (candle glow, dress, halo)	301	744
	= lt green (leaves, checkerboard)	1042	504
	= med green (stem border, leaves)	214	368
✦	= dk green (calyx)	216	502
	very dk green	217	561
	= lt turquoise (upper and lower dress)	185	964
	= med turquoise (upper and lower dress)	187	958
⊠	= dk turquoise (upper dress)	189	943
	= very lt blue (wings)	128	800
	= lt blue ("ANGEL," dress, flowers)	130	809
≈	= med blue ("ANGEL," dress, flowers)	131	798
	= med dk blue (dress)	132	797
▦	= very dk blue (dress)	149	311
	brown	355	975
✕	= lt rust (border, hair)	337	3776
	= med rust (hair)	338	922
	dk rust	351	400
	gray	400	317

╲ = Straight Stitch:
  inside of fan border—lt rust

│ = Backstitch:
  vine border, stems, leaves, small zigzag lines,
    A–D, Q–Z—very dk green
  blue/fuchsia triangle border near top—med blue
  "ANGELS," blue flowers, big zigzag lines, K–P,
    borderline around personalization—med dk blue
  saying—very dk blue
  inner borderlines, halo, candle, E–J—brown
  fan outlines—lt rust
  borderline below verse, hearts—med rust
  hair, skin—dk rust
  remaining outlines—gray

Shaded area shows last two rows from chart on page 74.

desired name, date, and / or message

Continue stitching from chart on page 77.

	page 74	page 75
	page 76	page 77

Shaded area shows last two rows from chart on page 75.

Shaded area shows last two rows from chart on page 76.

		Anchor	DMC
•	= white (wings)	1	blanc
	= lt fuchsia (sleeves, ribbon, triangles)	85	3609
□	= med fuchsia (sleeves, ribbon, rectangles)	86	3608
■	= dk fuchsia (ribbon)	87	3607
	= lt peach (skin)	778	3774
○	= med peach (border flowers, hearts)	8	3824
	= lt orange (candle glow, sleeve edge)	313	742
	= med orange (candle glow)	323	3825
	= dk orange (flame)	329	3340
	= lt yellow (halo, candle glow)	386	3823
✗	= med yellow (candle glow, dress, halo)	301	744
	= lt green (leaves, checkerboard)	1042	504
	= med green (stem border, leaves)	214	368
	= dk green (calyx)	216	502
	very dk green	217	561
	= lt turquoise (upper and lower dress)	185	964
	= med turquoise (upper and lower dress)	187	958
⊠	= dk turquoise (upper dress)	189	943
	= very lt blue (wings)	128	800
	= lt blue ("ANGEL," dress, flowers)	130	809
	= med blue ("ANGEL," dress, flowers)	131	798
	= med dk blue (dress)	132	797
	= very dk blue (dress)	149	311
	brown	355	975
※	= lt rust (border, hair)	337	3776
	= med rust (hair)	338	922
	dk rust	351	400
	gray	400	317

╲ = Straight Stitch:
    inside of fan border—lt rust

❘ = Backstitch:
    vine border, stems, leaves, small zigzag lines,
      A-D, Q-Z—very dk green
    blue/fuchsia triangle border near top—med blue
    "ANGELS," blue flowers, big zigzag lines, K-P,
      borderline around personalization—med dk blue
    saying—very dk blue
    inner borderlines, halo, candle, E-J—brown
    fan outlines—lt rust
    borderline below verse, hearts—med rust
    hair, skin—dk rust
    remaining outlines—gray

All Creatures Praise the Lord

Design size: 176 wide x 95 high

Photo: pages 22 and 23.

		Anchor	DMC
•	= white (diapers)	2	blanc
⊙	= lt pink (hearts, bird cheeks, hat ribbon)	25	3326
	= med pink (beaver shirt, diaper trim, hat ribbon)	27	899
⊙	= dk pink (beaver shirt, hat ribbon)	42	309
	= red (hearts, rainbow, flowers, rabbit shirt)	13	349
	= orange (rainbow, bird feet, flowers)	11	351
	= lt yellow (rainbow, sun, hat)	301	744

		Anchor	DMC
❖	= med yellow (sun, butterfly)	297	743
	= lt green (rainbow, leaves)	238	703
	= med green (leaves)	239	702
	dk green	923	699
	= turquoise (raccoon shirt)	186	959
	= lt blue (bird, rabbit pants, rainbow, "PRAISE THE LORD")	159	3325

Continue stitching from chart on page 79.

Photo model: stitched on a 18" x 13" piece of white 14-count Aida cloth.

		Anchor	DMC
=	med blue (bird, checkerboard, rabbit pants, "PRAISE THE LORD")	131	799
=	dk blue (bird, "PRAISE THE LORD")	137	798
=	very dk blue (border)	132	797
=	lt purple (flowers, bear shirt)	96	554
=	dk purple (flowers, rainbow)	98	553
=	tan (rabbit)	387	739
=	very lt rust (beaver, bear, rabbit)	881	945
=	lt rust (butterfly)	347	402
=	med rust (raccoon, butterfly, beaver)	349	922
	dk rust	352	400
=	brown (eyes)	381	938

		Anchor	DMC
■ =	black (raccoon)	403	310

| = Backstitch:
- pink shirt, pink hearts, hat ribbon—dk pink
- red hearts, red shirt, flowers, inner border outline—red
- sun rays, hat outline—orange
- leaves and stems—dk green
- clouds, letters, diapers, purple shirt, striped blue pans, turquoise shirt, bunny tail, bluebird (except breast)—very dk blue
- remaining tails, body outlines & ears, sun outline, bird beak, bird breast, bird feet, yellow butterfly—dk rust
- beaver face, bear eye and nose, bird eye—brown
- remaining butterfly—black

Shaded area shows last two rows from chart on page 78.

79

Continue stitching from chart on page 81.

Continue stitching from chart on page 82.

Water My Garden

Design size: 124 wide x 150 high

Photo model: stitched on a 15" x 17" piece of antique white 14-count Aida cloth.

Stitching notes: The bees are shown stitched with ribbon; refer to the seperate color key below and Ribbon Embroidery Directions on page 128.

Photo: pages 24 and 25.

		Anchor	DMC
•	= white (watering can, tulip, bird)	1	blanc
○	= lt pink (tulips)	36	3326
	= med pink (tulips)	38	961
	= dk pink (tulips)	42	326
⊠	= med red (tulips)	46	666
■	= dk red (watering can)	43	814
	= very lt fuschia (violets)	95	554
	= lt fuchsia (violets)	85	3609
♙	= dk fuchsia (violets)	94	917
	= lt orange (watering can)	313	742
	= med orange (watering can)	314	741
◉	= dk orange (watering can)	324	721
	= yellow (watering can)	300	745
▫	= lt yellow-green (leaves, stems)	253	472
	= med yellow-green (leaves, stems)	265	3347
▩	= dk yellow-green (leaves)	267	469
	= very dk yellow-green (leaves, stems)	268	937
	= med green (leaves)	225	702
✿	= dk green (leaves)	210	562
■	= very dk green (leaves)	683	890
	= very lt blue-green (leaves)	206	564
◔	= lt blue-green (leaves)	204	563
	= turquoise (blue flowers, leaves)	185	964
	= very lt blue (watering can)	120	3747
	= lt blue (watering can)	130	809
⊠	= med blue (watering can)	137	798
■	= dk blue (border)	139	797
▣	= blue-purple (lettering)	118	340
	= lt purple (lettering, violets)	108	210
✤	= med purple (violets)	109	209
▩	= dk purple (violets)	110	208
	= lt gray (bird, watering can)	398	415
	= dk gray (bird, watering can)	400	317
■	= black(bird, watering can)	403	310

- • = French Knots:
  - spout—dk gray
- | = Backstitch:
  - around eye—white
  - leaves, stems, reference—very dk yellow-green
  - violets, verse—dk purple
  - legs, feet, black part of bird, inside eye—black
  - tulips, watering can, remaining bird—dk gray

Ribbon Embroidery

◡	= loop stitch (wings)	white (7mm)
◠	= straight stitch (body)	yellow (7mm)
╲	= straight stitch (body stripe)	black (2mm)
		= backstitch (antennae)	black floss (2 strands)

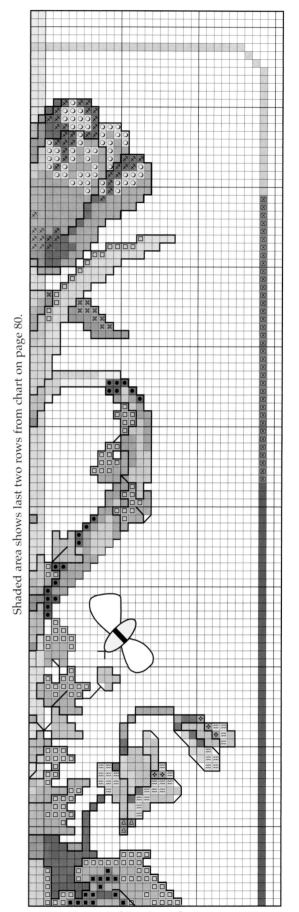

Shaded area shows last two rows from chart on page 80.

Continue stitching from chart on page 83.

Shaded area shows last two rows from chart on page 80.

Continue stitching from chart below.

Shaded area shows last two rows from chart on page 81.

Shaded area shows last two rows from above.

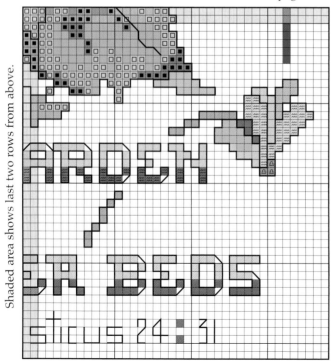

page 80	page 81
page 82 upper	page 82 lower

A Day Hemmed in Prayer

Design size: 100 wide x 69 high
Photo model: stitched on a 13″ x 11″ piece of natural 14-count Aida cloth.
Photo: pages 26 and 27.

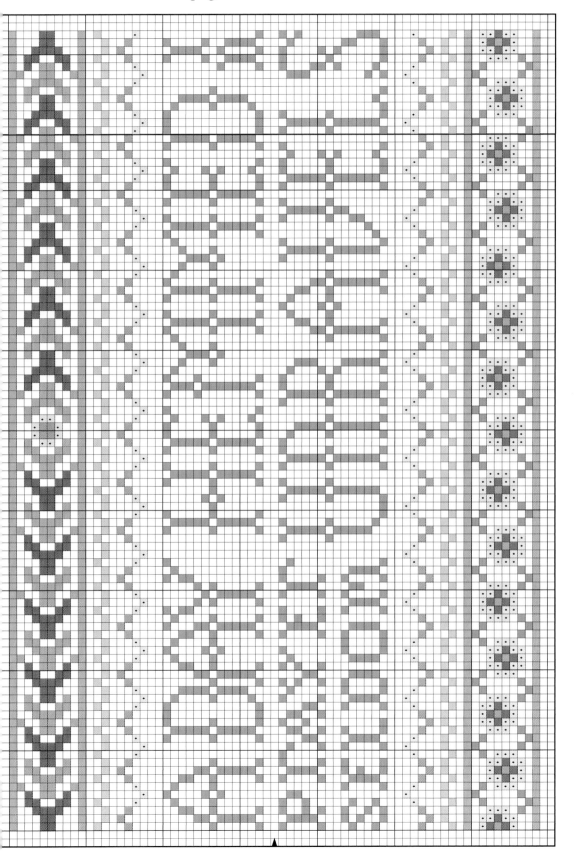

	Anchor	DMC	
·	74	3354	= lt pink (zigzag borders, flowers)
	76	961	= dk pink (zigzag borders, flowers)
	215	320	= lt green (center border)
	217	561	= dk green (floral border, lettering)
	130	809	= blue (both sides of outer borders)
	347	402	= lt brown (upper border)
	349	301	= med brown (upper border, flowers)

Lilies on the Cross

Design size: 82 wide x 110 high
Photo model: stitched on a 12" x 15" piece of cream 28-count Cashel linen.
Photo: pages 28 and 29.

		Anchor	DMC
•	= white (lilies)	1	blanc
	= lt yellow-green (leaves)	253	472
	= med yellow-green (leaves)	265	3347
	med dk yellow-green	267	469
	= dk yellow-green (leaves)	856	370
	= med green (leaves)	242	989
	= dk green (leaves)	210	562
	= lt blue (lilies)	928	3811
	= med blue (lilies)	1039	518
	= med turquoise (cross front)	433	996
	= dk turquoise (cross front)	169	806
	= lt blue-gray (cross side)	1033	932
	= dk blue-gray (cross)	1036	3750
	= med rust (lilies)	1048	3776
	= dk rust (cross)	1049	3826
	gray	400	317
	= gold braid (Kreinik #8 Braid, 002)		
	gold cable (Kreinik Cable, 002P)		

| = Backstitch:
 yellow-green leaves & stems—med dk yellow-green
 green leaves & stems—dk green
 stamens—dk rust
 cross, flowers—gray
 border patterns—gold cable

Bless Thy Beasts and Singing Birds

Design size: 94 wide x 176 high

Continue stitching from chart on page 87.

Photo model: stitched on a 13" x 18" piece of white 14-count Aida cloth.
Photo: pages 30 and 31.

	Anchor	DMC
= white (deer, raccoon, bunnies, bee)	2	blanc
= pink (bunny, deer, birds)	25	3326
= med red (flowers)	13	349
= dk red (inner border)	43	815
= orange (flowers)	324	721
= lt yellow large (butterfly)	301	744
= med yellow (butterfly, flower centers, bee)	297	743
= lt green (leaves, stems)	264	772
= med green (leaves)	208	563
= dk green (leaves)	210	562
= lt blue (birds)	167	519
= med blue (birds)	168	518
= dk blue (border, small butterflies)	132	797
= fuchsia (flowers)	86	3608
= tan (bunnies)	387	739
= very lt rust (bunnies, deer)	881	945
= lt rust (bunnies, deer, raccoon, birds)	347	402
= med rust (butterfly, raccoon)	349	922

	Anchor	DMC
= dk rust (butterfly, deer, raccoon)	352	400
= brown (bunny, bird, & deer eyes)	381	938
= lt gray (rock)	398	415
dk gray	400	317
= black (raccoon)	403	310

| = Backstitch:

red flowers, dk red border—dk red

leaves, flower stems, grass—dk green

vines & tendrils—dk green (2 strands)

border, bird outlines (except breasts),
      two small butterflies—dk blue

lettering—dk blue (2 strands)

animal outlines, yellow buterfly, faces, bird breasts,
      eyes and beaks—dk rust

bee wings & zoom, rock—dk gray

Shaded area shows last two rows from chart on page 86.

CONSIDER the LILIES of the field how they grow consider the lilies of the field how they grow

MATTHEW 6:28

Continue stitching from chart on page 89.

Consider the Lilies

Design size: 79 wide x 124 high

Photo model: stitched on an 11" x 14" piece of antique white 14-count Aida cloth.

Photo: pages 32 and 33.

		Anchor	DMC
■ = very lt red (flowers, lettering)		9	352
◨ = lt red (flowers, lettering)		11	351
■ = med red (flowers, lettering)		1025	347
dk red		1015	3777
▨ = very lt peach (flowers)		6	754
▢ = lt peach (flowers)		8	3824
▤ = very lt yellow-green (leaves, stems)		259	772
▨ = lt yellow-green (leaves, stems)		254	3348
▦ = med yellow-green (leaves, stems)		255	907
dk yellow-green		268	469
▥ = med green (leaves, stems)		257	905
■ = dk green (leaves, stems)		258	904

· = French Knots: med green

| = Backstitch:
 lower right border flowers—very lt red
 remaining flowers—dk red
 stems, leaves—dk yellow-green
 lettering—med green
 borderline—dk green

Shaded area shows last two rows from chart on page 88.

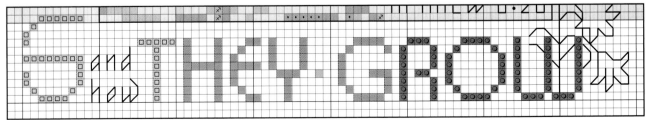

Whoever Eats My Bread

Design size: 63 wide x 91 high
Photo model: stitched on a 12″ x 14″ piece of natural 14-count Aida cloth.
Photo: pages 34 and 35.

		Anchor	DMC
○ = lt pink (hearts, corners)		23	3713
▣ = med pink (hearts, flowers)		36	3326
▪ = med peach (borders)		1023	3712
dk peach		1024	3328
▣ = lt gold (flowers, ribbon)		311	3827
▦ = med gold (zigzag lines, lower inner border)		363	436
▩ = dk gold (zigzag lines, ribbon)		365	435
very dk gold		310	780
✳ = lt green (leaves, wreaths)		265	3347
▩ = med green (leaves, wreaths)		267	469
dk green		268	937

| = Backstitch:
  zigzag line, flowers, "MY BREAD," hearts, single scallop line—dk peach
  gold band, ribbon band—dk gold
  "WHOEVER EATS"—very dk gold
  leaves, double scallop lines, "SING MY SONG," vine—dk green

91

Believe

Design size: 81 wide x 174 high
Photo model: stitched on a 12" x 18" piece of cream 28-count Quaker clot
Stitching notes: Use the large alphabet on page 124 to work initials in dk pink.
Photo: pages 36 and 37.

		Anchor	DMC
•	= white (wings)	1	blanc
	= lt pink (dress)	73	963
◎	= med pink (dress, border)	75	962
	= med dk pink (border)	76	961
■	= dk pink (dress)	77	3687
	= lt peach (skin)	778	3774
◻	= med peach (skin)	868	353
	= dk peach (letters)	8	3824
⊠	= med orange (border, halo, BELIEVE)	323	3825
■	= dk orange (background)	30	947
	= lt yellow (halo, hair)	386	3823
◇	= med yellow (halo, hair)	301	744
	= dk yellow (hair)	302	743
	= lt green (sash)	1043	369
	= med green (sash, letters)	240	966
	dk green	211	562
	= lt turquoise (sleeve, border)	928	3811
	= med turquoise (border, sleeve, letters)	186	959
■	= dk turquoise (border)	188	3812
	= lt blue (wings)	128	800

		Anchor	DMC
■	= med blue (letters, lamp)	129	809
■	= dk blue	131	798
	= lt purple (letters, flowers)	85	3609
◪	= med purple (letters)	109	209
	dk purple	111	553
■	= brown (lantern chain)	355	975
	gray	400	317

| = Backstitch:
  pink flower border, dress, pink letters, hearts—dk pink
  lattice outline, small orange flowers—dk orange
  green stem ends on blue/purple flowers, green shawl,
    green letters—dk green
  turquoise borders, four turquoise motifs at top, sleeves in dress
    turquoise zigzag between hearts, turquoise letters, floral
    pattern at bottom—dk turquoise
  wings, purple flowers, blue letters—dk blue
  sleeve lining, purple letters—dk purple
  "BELIEVE," bells and bell cord, halo, hair, skin, face, rope,
    peach and yellow letters, tie strings on shawl—brown
  lantern, tassel—gray

Continue stitching from chart on page 93.

initials

93

Give Thanks to God

Design size: 116 wide x 159 high

Photo model: stitched on a 15" x 18" piece of white 14-count Aida cloth.

Stitching notes: On the letters that are worked with both cross stitches and backstitches, backstitch around the cross stitches with one strand of floss then backstitch the line extensions with two strands of floss.

Photo: pages 38 and 39.

Continue stitching from chart on page 96.

| page 94 | page 95 |
| page 96 | page 97 |

Shaded area shows last two rows from chart on page 94.

Continue stitching from chart on page 97.

		Anchor	DMC
•	= white (clouds, diaper, bunny muzzle, raccoon, lamb)	2	blanc
○	= lt pink (flowers, bunny ears, bird, lamb & bunny cheeks)	25	3326
	= med pink (hat flower, "Give thanks... lettering, small hearts)	42	335
	= med red (hearts, rainbow, house, "Give thanks... lettering)	13	349
	= dk red (door)	43	815
	= peach ("Thank you God... lettering, flowers)	8	352
□	= lt yellow (bunny, muzzles - except bunny)	387	739
	= med yellow (rainbow, hat, raccoon shirt)	301	744
	= dk yellow (raccoon shirt, hat, sun, flower, flower centers)	297	743
	= lt green (flower leaves, bushes, trees)	264	772
	= med green (flower stems, rainbow, leaves, bushes)	238	703
	= dk green (outer border, "Give thanks... border, "Thank you... lettering)	212	561
	= med turquoise (bear pants & shirt, rainbow)	186	959
	= dk turquoise (bear shirt, lamb collar)	187	958
	= lt aqua (butterfly, bird, watering can flowers)	167	519
	= dk aqua (butterfly, bird)	168	518
	= lt blue (overalls, rainbow section lettering, butterfly)	130	809
	= dk blue (rainbow section border, butterfly)	132	797
	= lt purple (bow)	108	211
	= dk purple (bow, hat flower)	98	553
	= magenta (heart with bow)	86	3608
	= very lt rust (bears, cat, bunny feet)	881	945
	= lt rust (bears, raccoons, cat)	347	402
	= med rust (raccoons, tree trunks)	349	922
	= dk rust (raccoons)	352	400
	= brown (eyes)	381	938
	= lt gray (lamb)	398	415
	dk gray	400	317
■	= black (raccoon)	403	310

| = Backstitch:
   pink flowers—med pink
   pink lettering—med pink (1 & 2 strands)
   red/peach butterfly—med red
   cursive backstitched lettering in rainbow section—med red (2 strands)
   "Give Thanks to God"—med red (1 & 2 strands)
   hearts, peach flowers, schoolhouse, heart strings, magenta flower & shirt, hat flower—dk red
   "A true friend...God"—dk red (2 strands)
   "God" in rainbow section, peach & magenta lettering—dk red (1 & 2 strands)
   diapers—lt blue
   blue & purple butterflies, blue flowers, bluebird (except breast), purple ribbon, blue overalls, lamb collar, turquoise shirt & pants—dk blue
   upper right zigzag border—dk blue (2 strands)
   blue lettering—dk blue (1 & 2 strands)
   stems & leaves, hills & trees—dk green
   middle right zigzag border, vine border, "Thank you...everything" —dk green (2 strands)
   green lettering—dk green (1 & 2 strands)
   bear, raccoon & bunny outlines, eyes and mouths, yellow shirt, hat, yellow flowers, sun, tree trunks, bottom half of yellow butterfly, bluebird breast, beak & eye—dk rust
   yellow lettering—dk rust (1 & 2 strands)
   lamb eye—brown
   clouds, watering can, lamb—dk gray
   top half of yellow butterfly—black

page 94	page 95
page 96	page 97

Shaded area shows last two rows from chart on page 94.

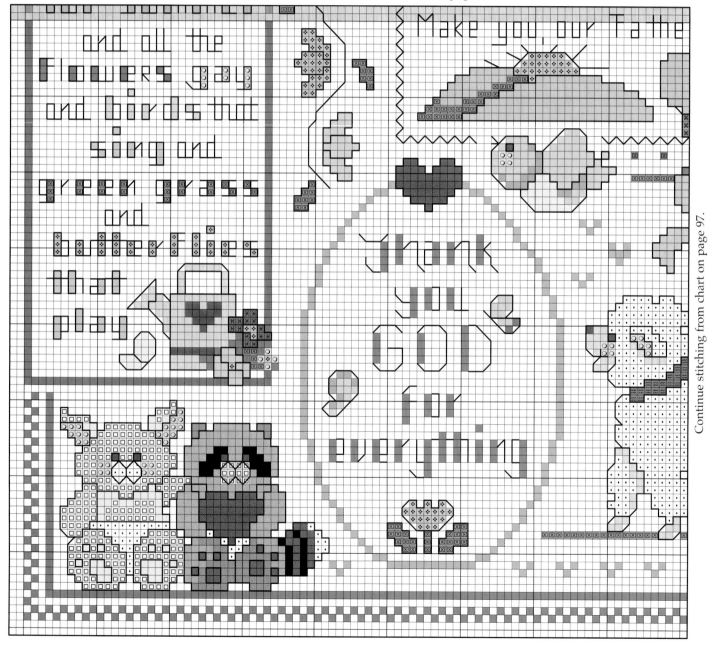

Continue stitching from chart on page 97.

	Anchor	DMC
· = white (clouds, diaper, bunny muzzle, raccoon, lamb)	2	blanc
◦ = lt pink (flowers, bunny ears, bird, lamb & bunny cheeks)	25	3326
▨ = med pink (hat flower, "Give thanks... lettering, small hearts)	42	335
▨ = med red (hearts, rainbow, house, "Give thanks... lettering)	13	349
▨ = dk red (door)	43	815
▨ = peach ("Thank you God... lettering, flowers)	8	352
□ = lt yellow (bunny, muzzles - except bunny)	387	739
▨ = med yellow (rainbow, hat, raccoon shirt)	301	744
✿ = dk yellow (raccoon shirt, hat, sun, flower, flower centers)	297	743
▨ = lt green (flower leaves, bushes, trees)	264	772
⊠ = med green (flower stems, rainbow, leaves, bushes)	238	703
▨ = dk green (outer border, "Give thanks... border, "Thank you... lettering)	212	561
⊠ = med turquoise (bear pants & shirt, rainbow)	186	959
▨ = dk turquoise (bear shirt, lamb collar)	187	958
▨ = lt aqua (butterfly, bird, watering can flowers)	167	519
▨ = dk aqua (butterfly, bird)	168	518
▨ = lt blue (overalls, rainbow section lettering, butterfly)	130	809
▨ = dk blue (rainbow section border, butterfly)	132	797
▨ = lt purple (bow)	108	211
▨ = dk purple (bow, hat flower)	98	553
⋈ = magenta (heart with bow)	86	3608
▨ = very lt rust (bears, cat, bunny feet)	881	945
▨ = lt rust (bears, raccoons, cat)	347	402
⌘ = med rust (raccoons, tree trunks)	349	922
▨ = dk rust (raccoons)	352	400
▨ = brown (eyes)	381	938
▨ = lt gray (lamb)	398	415
dk gray	400	317
■ = black (raccoon)	403	310

| = Backstitch:

pink flowers—med pink

pink lettering—med pink (1 & 2 strands)

red / peach butterfly—med red

cursive backstitched lettering in rainbow section—med red (2 strands)

"Give Thanks to God"—med red (1 & 2 strands)

hearts, peach flowers, schoolhouse, heart strings, magenta flower & shirt, hat flower—dk red

"A true friend...God"—dk red (2 strands)

"God" in rainbow section, peach & magenta lettering—dk red (1 & 2 strands)

diapers—lt blue

blue & purple butterflies, blue flowers, bluebird (except breast), purple ribbon, blue overalls, lamb collar, turquoise shirt & pants—dk blue

upper right zigzag border—dk blue (2 strands)

blue lettering—dk blue (1 & 2 strands)

stems & leaves, hills & trees—dk green

middle right zigzag border, vine border, "Thank you...everything" —dk green (2 strands)

green lettering—dk green (1 & 2 strands)

bear, raccoon & bunny outlines, eyes and mouths, yellow shirt, hat, yellow flowers, sun, tree trunks, bottom half of yellow butterfly, bluebird breast, beak & eye—dk rust

yellow lettering—dk rust (1 & 2 strands)

lamb eye—brown

clouds, watering can, lamb—dk gray

top half of yellow butterfly—black

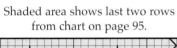

Shaded area shows last two rows from chart on page 95.

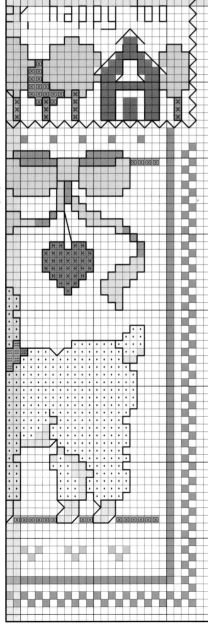

Shaded area shows last two rows from chart on page 96.

Land of Oil-Olive and Honey

Design size: 99 wide x 120 high
Photo model: stitched on a 14" x 15" piece of antique white 14-count Aida cloth.
Photo: pages 40 and 41.

		Anchor	DMC
·	= white (bees)	1	blanc
	= lt red (bees)	9	352
	= med red (pomegranates)	11	351
	= dk red (pomegranates)	1025	347
	very dk red	1015	3777
	yellow	297	973
◦	= very lt green (leaves)	259	772
	= lt green (leaves)	265	3347
	= med green (leaves)	266	471
	= med dk green (leaves)	267	469
	= dk green (leaves)	268	937
	very dk green	269	936
	= very lt purple (grapes)	869	3743
	= lt purple (grapes)	870	3042
	= med purple (grapes)	872	3740
	dk purple	873	327
○	= very lt tan (hive)	852	3047
	= lt tan (hive, wheat)	372	738
	= med tan (hive, wheat)	373	3828
	= med dk tan (hive)	375	869
	= dk tan (hive)	889	610
	very dk tan	906	829
	= taupe (border)	832	612
	= gray (blackberries)	235	414
	= black (bees, blackberries)	403	310
	= French Knots: dk purple		
|	= Backstitch:		

    pomegranates—very dk red
    bee stripes—yellow (2 strands)
    med and dk green leaf veins—very lt green
    remaining veins, remaining leaf outlines, remaining stems—very dk green
    grapes, lettering—dk purple
    wheat—med dk tan
    hive, olive branches—very dk tan
    bees, olives—black

FOR

THE LORD THY GOD

BRINGETH THEE INTO A GOOD LAND

A LAND OF WHEAT, AND BARLEY,

AND VINES, AND FIG TREES,

AND POMEGRANATES,

A LAND OF

OIL-OLIVE AND HONEY

DEUTERONOMY 8:7-8

Continue stitching from chart on page 101.

Continue stitching from chart on page 102.

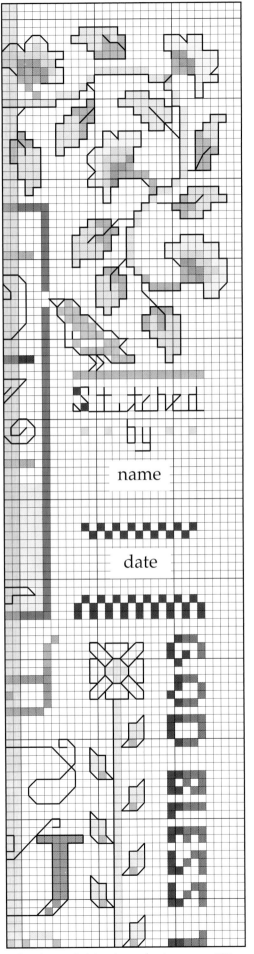

Shaded area shows last two rows from chart on page 100.

name

date

Continue stitching from chart on page 103.

Each Day is a New Beginning

Design size: 115 wide x 156 high

Photo model: stitched on a 15" x 18" piece of antique white 14-count Aida cloth.

Stitching notes: Use the alphabet and numerals on page 124 to add name of stitcher and date with dk brown.

Photo: pages 42 and 43.

		Anchor	DMC
▨ = lt peach (flowers)		1022	760
▨ = med peach (lettering)		1023	3712
▨ = dk peach (flowers, lettering, wheat)		1024	3328
= very lt yellow (background)		275	746
= lt yellow (flowers, wheat, sun)		300	745
= med yellow (flowers)		301	744
= med dk yellow (sun)		891	676
▨ = dk yellow (wheat, sun)		306	783
▨ = very dk yellow (sun)		308	781
= lt green (leaves, stems)		214	368
▨ = med green (leaves, stems)		216	502
▨ = dk green (wheat)		218	319
= lt blue (background, borders, near "by")		120	3747
= lt blue (1 strand) (background)		120	3747
▨ = med blue (lettering, background, near "stitched," near pot)		121	809
▨ = dk blue (borders, numbers)		122	3807
very dk blue		123	820
▨ = lt brown (wheat)		368	437
▨ = med brown (lettering)		369	435
▪ = dk brown (lines near name & date, lettering)		355	975
▨ = lt rust (pot)		1047	402
▨ = dk rust (wheat, pot)		1048	3776
▨ = gray (birds)		1041	844

✕ = Large Cross Stitches:
    top border—med brown
    inside verse—dk brown

| = Backstitch:
    flowers (except yellow daisies),
           "Beginning"—dk peach
    leaves, stems—dk green
    A, D, G, J, M, P, S, V, Y—dk blue
    B, E, H, K, N, Q, T, W, Z, numerals—very dk blue
    C, F, I, L, O, R, U, X, "one," "time,"
          "Stitched by," brown wheat, flower pots,
          sun, yellow daisies—dk brown
    yellow wheat—dk rust
    birds—gray

| page 100 | page 101 |
| page 102 | page 103 |

Shaded area shows last two rows from chart on page 100.

Continue stitching from chart on page 103.

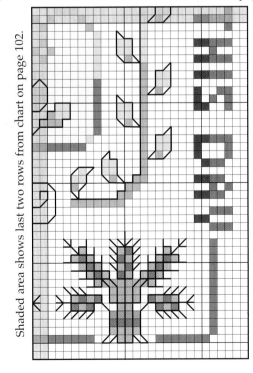

Shaded area shows last two rows from chart on page 102.

aded area shows last two rows from chart on page 101.

		Anchor	DMC
▨ =	lt peach (flowers)	1022	760
▨ =	med peach (lettering)	1023	3712
▨ =	dk peach (flowers, lettering, wheat)	1024	3328
=	very lt yellow (background)	275	746
=	lt yellow (flowers, wheat, sun)	300	745
=	med yellow (flowers)	301	744
▨ =	med dk yellow (sun)	891	676
▨ =	dk yellow (wheat, sun)	306	783
▨ =	very dk yellow (sun)	308	781
=	lt green (leaves, stems)	214	368
▨ =	med green (leaves, stems)	216	502
▨ =	dk green (wheat)	218	319
▨ =	lt blue (background, borders, near "by")	120	3747
=	lt blue (1 strand) (background)	120	3747
▨ =	med blue (lettering, background, near "stitched," near pot)	121	809
▨ =	dk blue (borders, numbers)	122	3807
	very dk blue	123	820
▨ =	lt brown (wheat)	368	437
▨ =	med brown (lettering)	369	435
▨ =	dk brown (lines near name & date, lettering)	355	975
▨ =	lt rust (pot)	1047	402
▨ =	dk rust (wheat, pot)	1048	3776
▨ =	gray (birds)	1041	844

✕ = Large Cross Stitches:
    top border—med brown
    inside verse—dk brown

| = Backstitch:
    flowers (except yellow daisies),
            "Beginning"—dk peach
    leaves, stems—dk green
    A, D, G, J, M, P, S, V, Y—dk blue
    B, E, H, K, N, Q, T, W, Z, numerals—very dk blue
    C, F, I, L, O, R, U, X, "one," "time,"
            "Stitched by," brown wheat, flower pots,
            sun, yellow daisies—dk brown
    yellow wheat—dk rust
    birds—gray

Welcome Angels

Design size: 110 wide x 154 high

Photo model: stitched on a 14″ x 17″ piece of light mocha 28-count Quaker cloth.

Photo: pages 44 and 45.

Continue stitching from chart on page 105.

Continue stitching from chart on page 106.

Shaded area shows last two rows from chart on page 104.

Continue stitching from chart on page 107.

	Anchor	DMC
· = cream (wings, "WELCOME" & hearts background, windows)	275	746
▫ = lt pink (dresses, cheeks, large heart)	894	223
⊠ = med pink (roof, small hearts, dresses)	895	3722
▦ = dk pink (small hearts, roof, door, dresses, large heart)	896	3721
▨ = peach (skin)	1012	754
○ = yellow (wings)	301	744
gold	901	3829
▦ = lt green (checkerboard border)	842	3013
▦ = med green (checkerboard border, bushes)	843	3012
▦ = dk green (bushes, arch, lower border)	262	3363
▦ = lt blue (house)	129	800
▦ = med blue (dresses)	121	809
▦ = dk blue ("WELCOME," house, background)	122	3807
▦ = brown (hair)	360	898

〇 = Lazy Daisies:
   flower leaves on dresses—dk green (2 strands)
   alphabet & verse tracery—dk blue (2 strands)

• = French Knots: dk blue

| = Backstitch:
   pink dress outlines, apron outline on blue dress—dk pink
   mouths, zigzag on blue dress, inner border around verse,
     pink leaf stems above heart—dk pink (2 strands)
   halos—gold (2 strands)
   remaining stems—dk green (2 strands)
   upper half of alphabet, borderlines around
     three angels—med blue (2 strands)
   window panes, blue dress outline, apron outlines on
     pink dresses—dk blue
   zigzags on pink dresses, verse, reference—dk blue (2 strands)
   hands, wings—brown
   hair, eyes—brown (2 strands)

❚ = Backstitch: dk blue (2 strands)

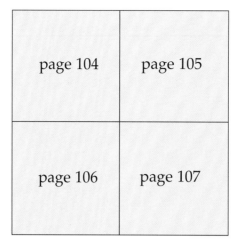

Continue stitching from chart on page 107.

Shaded area shows last two rows from chart on page 104.

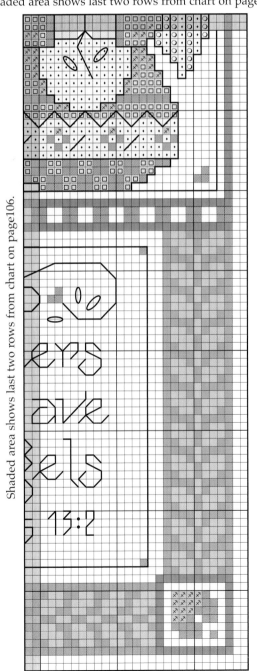

Shaded area shows last two rows from chart on page 105.

Shaded area shows last two rows from chart on page106.

	Anchor	DMC
• = cream (wings, "WELCOME" & hearts background, windows)	275	746
□ = lt pink (dresses, cheeks, large heart)	894	223
⊠ = med pink (roof, small hearts, dresses)	895	3722
▨ = dk pink (small hearts, roof, door, dresses, large heart)	896	3721
▦ = peach (skin)	1012	754
○ = yellow (wings)	301	744
gold	901	3829
▨ = lt green (checkerboard border)	842	3013
▨ = med green (checkerboard border, bushes)	843	3012
▨ = dk green (bushes, arch, lower border)	262	3363
▨ = lt blue (house)	129	800
▨ = med blue (dresses)	121	809
▨ = dk blue ("WELCOME," house, background)	122	3807
▨ = brown (hair)	360	898

ʘ = Lazy Daisies:
    flower leaves on dresses—dk green (2 strands)
    alphabet & verse tracery—dk blue (2 strands)

• = French Knots: dk blue

| = Backstitch:
    pink dress outlines, apron outline on blue dress—dk pink
    mouths, zigzag on blue dress, inner border around verse,
       pink leaf stems above heart—dk pink (2 strands)
    halos—gold (2 strands)
    remaining stems—dk green (2 strands)
    upper half of alphabet, borderlines around
       three angels—med blue (2 strands)
    window panes, blue dress outline, apron outlines on
       pink dresses—dk blue
    zigzags on pink dresses, verse, reference—dk blue (2 strands)
    hands, wings—brown
    hair, eyes—brown (2 strands)

| = Backstitch: dk blue (2 strands)

Send Out Fragrance

Design size: 112 wide x 107 high
Photo model: stitched on a 15" x 14" piece of antique white 14-count Aida cloth.

Continue stitching from chart on page 109.

Stitching notes: Ribbon embroidery is used for the following areas: the couched border, corner motifs, and bow on main stem. Refer to the separate color key below and General Directions, Ribbon Embroidery, page 128. To finish bow, turn under raw end of each streamer and secure with last French Knot.

Photo: pages 46 and 47.

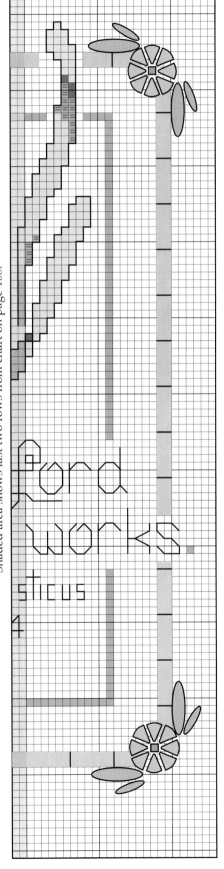

Shaded area shows last two rows from chart on page 108.

		Anchor	DMC
·	= white (flowers)	1	blanc
▨	= med peach (flower centers)	11	351
▣	= dk peach (flower centers)	13	347
○	= very lt yellow (flowers)	275	746
	= med yellow (flowers centers)	295	726
●	= dk yellow (flower centers)	303	742
▥	= lt gold (flowers)	886	677
■	= dk gold (stem)	888	3045
	= lt green (stem, leaves)	240	966
▨	= med green (stem, leaves)	242	989
▦	= dk green (stem, leaves)	244	702
▨	= med blue (lettering)	129	809
■	= dk blue (lettering)	131	798
▨	= med purple (border)	109	209
	dk purple	110	208

| = Backstitch:
    yellow flower centers—med peach
    gold area of stem, flowers—dk gold
    remaining stems, leaves—dk green
    reference, "Send...Fragrance,"—dk blue
    "for all his works"—med purple (2 strands)
    "bless the Lord"—dk purple (2 strands)

Ribbon Embroidery

▽	= loop stitch (flower petals)	lt peach (4mm)
▪	= French knot (flower center)	dk peach (4mm)
╱	= straight stitch (leaves)	green (4mm)
❘	= couching (border)	lt blue (4mm)
	couching (border)	dk blue floss (1 strand)
▭	= couching (bow)	lt purple (4mm)
	french knot (bow)	dk purple floss

Consider the Wondrous Works

Design size: 70 wide x 102 high
Photo model: stitched on a 12" x 14" piece of natural 14-count Aida cloth.
Photo: pages 48 and 49.

	Anchor	DMC
• = lt pink (lettering, pink line)	66	3688
▨ = med pink (lettering, top border, hearts)	68	3687
▨ = dk pink (lettering, hearts, butterflies, lower border)	65	3685
▥ = green (green lines, stems)	859	523
○ = lt purple (butterflies, flowers)	108	210
▨ = med purple (butterflies, flowers)	109	209
| = Backstitch:		
antennae—dk pink		
remaining outlines—med purple		

Design size: 76 wide x 145 high

For the preaching of the cross

Continue stitching from chart on page 113.

Photo model: stitched on a 12" x 17" piece of antique white 14-count Aida cloth.
Photo: pages 50 and 51.

		Anchor	DMC
•	= white (center & bottom borders)	1	blanc
■	= red (bow)	1014	355
▦	= fuchsia (cross)	86	3607
▫	= lt peach (roses)	6	754
▨	= med peach (bow, bottom border)	868	353
▪	= dk peach (roses)	9	352
⊠	= lt orange (yellow roses)	323	3825
◆	= dk orange (bow, roses)	326	720
	= lt yellow (yellow roses)	300	745
○	= med yellow (yellow roses)	305	743
▨	= dk yellow (center rose)	311	3827
▨	= gold (center rose)	945	834
▨	= yellow-green (leaves)	254	3348
▨	= med green (leaves)	243	703
■	= dk green (leaves)	246	986
▨	= lt turquoise (center borders)	185	964
▨	= dk turquoise (upper, center		
	& lower borders)	187	958
▨	= very lt orchid (cross)	95	3609
▣	= lt orchid (cross, butterfly)	96	3608
✳	= med orchid (cross)	97	554
■	= dk orchid (cross, bow)	98	553
▨	= med purple (cross)	110	208
	dk purple	101	550
	brown	358	801
▤	= lt rust (stems)	347	402
▨	= med rust (stems)	349	301
	gray	401	413

● = French Knots:
  reference—dk purple
  verse—brown

| = Backstitch:
  leaves (except brown leaf). stems—dk green
  purple flowers, small crosses, reference—dk purple
  branches, peach roses, brown leaf, verse—brown
  yellow roses—med rust
  white lattice, butterfly—gray

Shaded area shows last two rows from chart on page 112.

Music is a Gift from God

Design size: 133 wide x 82 high

Photo model: stitched on a 14″ x 11″ piece of white 14-count Aida cloth.

Photo: pages 52 and 53.

Continue stitching from chart on page 115.

	Anchor	DMC
· = white (wings)	1	blanc
▨ = lt pink (roses)	73	963
◙ = med pink (roses)	25	3326
▦ = dk pink (roses)	38	961
✻ = lt yellow (hair, dress)	300	745
▨ = med yellow (dress)	302	742
▦ = dk yellow (bell)	891	676
▨ = lt green (leaves)	225	702
▦ = med green (leaves)	227	701
dk green	923	699
▨ = lt turquoise (dress)	185	964
▦ = dk turquoise (dress)	187	958
▫ = lt blue (sheet music)	128	800
▦ = med blue (sheet music)	145	809
▦ = dk blue (notes)	131	798
very dk blue	147	797
▨ = lt purple (flowers, dress)	95	554
▦ = med purple (dress)	96	3608
dk purple	99	552
▨ = lt rust (hair, horn, harp)	336	402
▨ = med rust (hair, horn, harp)	338	922
dk rust	339	920
▨ = lt tan (skin)	778	945
≋ = med tan (skin)	868	353
▨ = lt brown (violin)	378	841
▦ = med brown (violin)	936	632
dk brown	360	898
▨ = lt gray (bell)	397	762
▦ = dk gray (bell)	399	318

· = French Knots: dk rust

\ = Straight Stitch: med brown

| = Backstitch:
  pink flowers, mouths—dk pink
  leaves, stems—dk green
  wings, sheet music, staff, notes,
      turquoise dress—very dk blue
  purple flowers, purple dress—dk purple
  hair, faces (except eyes), arms & legs,
      yellow dress, horn, harp, lettering,
      yellow bell—dk rust
  eyes, violin, harp strings—dk brown
  bow—dk brown (2 strands)
  gray bell—med gray

Shaded area shows last two rows from chart on page 114.

Angels Gather Here

Design size: 130 wide x 102 high

Photo model: stitched on a 17"x 15" piece of antique white 28-count Cashel linen. (stitched over two threads)

Photo: pages 54 and 55.

	= cream (wings)	275	746
⚙	= pink (cheeks)	49	3689
◼	= med red (dress)	335	606
◼	= dk red (dress)	47	321
	= med fuchsia (ribbon)	86	3608
◼	= dk fuchsia (ribbon)	88	718
	= lt peach (skin)	778	3774
·	= med peach (skin)	868	353
○	= lt orange (border, ribbon)	311	3827
⊠	= med orange (ribbon, halo)	313	742
◼	= dk orange (sleeves)	314	741
	= yellow (ribbon, halo)	300	745
	= med green (dress)	209	913
◼	= dk green (dress, border)	211	562
	= med blue (letters)	129	809
◼	= dk blue (letters)	131	798
	= lt purple (sleeve)	95	554
◆	= med purple (letters, sleeve)	96	3609
◼	= dk purple (letters)	99	552
▫	= lt rust (wings)	361	738
▦	= med rust (hair)	1003	922
⌘	= med lt rust (wings)	363	436
❖	= dk rust (hair)	1049	3826
	brown	355	975
	gray	400	317

• = French Knots: dk green

| = Backstitch:
    med red motif—med red
    "Angels Gather here"—dk fuchsia
    borderline, green area on corner motifs,
        two lines below French Knot—dk green
    blue letters—dk blue
    purple letters, remainder of corner motifs—dk purple
    small orange corners, wings, halo, hair, face,
        skin, ribbon—brown
    dress—gray

For Gifts Beyond Counting

Design size: 98 wide x 70 high

Photo model: stitched on a 14" x 12" piece of natural 14-count Aida cloth.

Photo: pages 56 and 57.

		Anchor	DMC
= lt green (center border)		214	368
= med green (vines)		216	502
m = blue-green (outer & inner borders)		779	3809
s = lt blue (blue border)		120	3747
= med blue (blue border, lettering)		121	809
= dk blue (blue border, lettering)		122	3807
= Backstitch:			
lettering—dk blue			
remaining outlines—blue-green			

Continue stitching from chart on page 119.

Shaded area shows last two rows from chart on page 118.

Bless Our Home

Design size: 104 wide x 128 high

Photo model: stitched on a 14" x 16" piece of antique white 14-count Aida cloth.

Stitching notes: Use the alphabet and numerals on page 124 to work family name and date with dk purple.

Photo: pages 58 and 59.

		Anchor	DMC
•	= white (house)	1	blanc
◦	= cream (center crosses)	275	746
▨	= very lt peach (corner & small crosses)	933	543
▨	= lt peach (house)	1021	761
▨	= fuschia (flowers)	96	3609
	= yellow (house, flowers)	301	744
▨	= lt green (leaves, grass)	1043	369
▨	= med green (leaves, tree)	240	966
▪	= dk green (leaves)	243	703
	very dk green	246	986
▣	= lt turquoise (lettering)	185	964
▪	= med turquoise (lettering)	187	958
	dk turquoise	189	943
	= very lt blue (sky)	1037	3756
▨	= med blue (wreath)	129	809
▪	= dk blue (border)	131	798
▨	= lt purple (flowers)	342	211
▨	= med purple (flowers, period)	109	209
	dk purple	111	553
▨	= lt rust (house)	372	738
▨	= med rust (house)	373	3828
	dk rust	357	433
	gray	400	317
▪	= copper (borders) (Kreinik #8 Braid, 021)		
	gold (or metallic gold thread) (Kreinik Cord, 002)		
•	= French Knots: dk rust		
|	= Backstitch:		

leaves, tendrils, trees, verse—very dk green

"Bless..Home," lower corner boxes—dk turquiose

flowers (except centers), "EST"—dk purple

roof, path, flower centers, four crosses in corners,
   large center cross, reference, three small crosses—dk rust

remaining house, round blue border,
   remaining crosses—gray

center & border filagrees, center circle in two
   small crosses—gold cord

Continue stitching from chart on page 121.

name

Shaded area shows last two rows from chart on page 120.

LET THE
FOUNDATIONS
THEREOF
BE
STRONGLY
LAID
EZRA 6:3

date

Expect a Miracle

Design size: 70 wide x 98 high
Photo model: stitched on a 12" x 14" piece of antique white 14-count Aida cloth.
Photo: pages 60 and 61.

		Anchor	DMC
·	= lt pink (upper flowers, lettering)	40	956
▒	= med pink (upper & lower flowers, center band, lettering)	39	309
▓	= dk pink (upper flowers, lettering)	43	815
✳	= lt yellow (flowers)	300	745
▫	= med yellow (flowers)	311	3827
▪	= lt green (leaves, stems, acorn band)	215	320
▒	= dk green (leaves, stems)	217	561
▒	= purple (upper purple bands)	872	3740
○	= lt rust (upper flowers, acorns)	347	402
▒	= med rust (acorns)	349	301
■	= dk rust (acorns)	358	801
X	= Large Cross Stitches: purple		
I	= Backstitch:		
	diamond shapes—lt green (2 strands)		
	yellow flowers, acorn stems—med rust		

Alphabets and Numerals

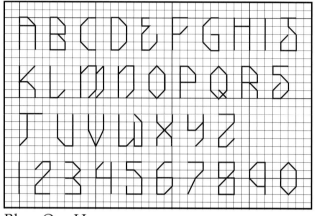

Bless Our Home

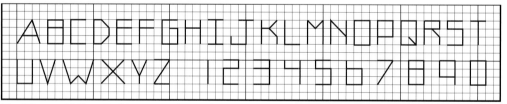

To Those Who Believe in Angels

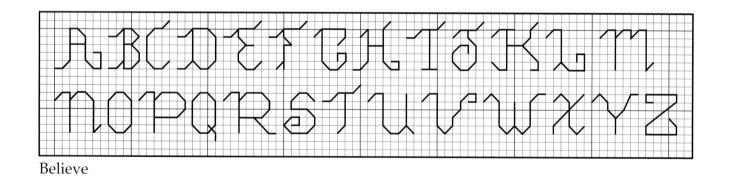

Believe

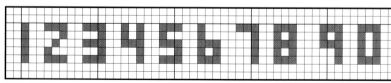

Each Day is a New Beginning

The Cross Stitch How-To

For many years, cross stitch has reigned as one of the most popular of needlework skills. It certainly deserves that popularity because it is quick and easy to do. It can be learned in less than a minute, and the materials for it are fairly inexpensive.

Counted cross stitch is worked by counting threads on blank even weave fabric; hence the term counted cross stitch. The designs are printed as graphs or charts, and the stitcher is able to reproduce the design by following the chart and transferring the pattern onto the fabric.

Each square on the chart represents one stitch, and the symbol (or color) on the chart indicates which floss color is to be used. A color key, which lists the symbols or colors used and the embroidery floss represented by that symbol, accompanies each chart. When a color key gives a color name but no symbol, that color is intended for backstitching or a decorative stitch explained on page 127.

What You Need for Cross Stitch

Fabrics

All counted cross stitch embroidery is worked on a fabric that is woven with the same number of vertical and horizontal threads (or blocks of threads) per inch. These fabrics are called "Even weave fabrics." The stitches are made over the intersections of horizontal and vertical threads (or over the blocks of threads). Since there is the same number of threads in each direction, each stitch is the same size and perfectly square.

The size of the completed design is determined by the number of stitches per inch of the even weave fabric. The more stitches per inch of the fabric, the smaller the design will be. Although the size fabric used to create the photographed model is given for each cross stitch piece, you can work the design on any count of fabric. If you choose to work your design on a lower thread count, the final design will be larger. You will therefore need a bigger piece of fabric.

Most of the designs in this book are shown on the most popular cross stitch fabric, 14-count. On a 14-count fabric, the designs are stitched over one thread. Some of the designs are stitched on 28-count fabrics where the design is worked over two threads. Both types of fabrics will produce a design that is 14 stitches per inch.

If you have never worked on 28-count linen, be sure to read the paragraph on working over two threads on page 127.

Threads

Six-strand embroidery floss is most commonly used for counted cross stitch. The six strands can be divided so that you can work with one, two or more strands at a time. Two strands of floss are usually used for all cross stitches and French Knots unless the specific color key indicates differently. Backstitches and straight stitches are worked with one strand unless otherwise noted.

Companies that manufacture floss have several hundred colors with different shades for almost every color. In addition, these companies introduce new colors fairly often. In order to identify these colors, floss companies use different color numbers for each color and each shade of a color.

Two of the largest floss companies are Anchor and DMC. While the cross stitch designs in this book were stitched in Anchor, we give the floss numbers for both Anchor and DMC. Since both Anchor and DMC have their own color range, the floss numbers may not be perfect color matches. They will, however, work for a specific design. If you feel that the color exchanges are not working, feel free to change them.

General color names for each of the threads used in a design are given in the color key. If there is only one red in a design, it will be called red, but if there are several, they will be called lt, med, and dk to represent light, medium and dark. The name of a particular color is not important; it is the symbol that tells you exactly which color of floss is to be used.

In addition to floss, several of the designs have the added sparkle of #8 braid and Cable manufactured by Kreinik©. Use only one strand of both Cable and metallic braid.

Needles

A blunt-point tapestry needle is used for counted cross stitch. The needle does not go through the threads but rather slips between them.

The fabric being used to make the project determines the required needle size. The smaller the needle, the higher the needle number will be. If you are using the correct size needle, it should be easy to thread with the thread indicated for that project. In addition, the needle should not distort the holes in the fabric but should be able to slip through the fabric easily. Size 24 or size 26 tapestry needles are suitable for all of the designs in this book.

Hoops, Frames and Scissors

The use of a hoop for counted cross stitch is purely optional and depends upon your personal preference. Many stitchers—especially those who work on linen—prefer to stitch without a hoop. These stitchers use the fingers of their left hand as a frame and stitch using a sewing stitch motion rather than the stab stitching that is used with hoops.

You can choose to use a hoop that is large enough to fit the entire design, or a small hoop that will just cover the area on which you are working. Be careful when you place the hoop over a small area. If the hoop sits on completed stitches, it may distort them slightly, but if you gently stroke the stitches with your needle, they will return to their original shape. If you use a hoop, center the hoop on the fabric with the screw in the 10 o'clock position if you are right hand-ed, or in the 2 o'clock position if you are left handed. Make sure that the fabric is taut; then tighten the screw. At the end of a day's stitching, be sure to remove the fabric from the hoop. Otherwise you may leave marks that will be almost impossible to remove from your stitched piece.

A scroll-type wooden frame or stretcher bars are prob-ably the best products to use to create the smoothest stitching without distorting the background fabric. They will hold the fabric taut throughout the stitching process. It takes time to learn to use a frame or stretch-er bars, but the final results will be worth your effort.

You will also want to have a small pair of sharp embroidery scissors with you at all times while you are working. The scissors can be used to cut your floss, or to snip mistakes if you make them.

Charts

The key to counted cross stitch is the chart (or graph) because the chart will show you exactly where to put the stitch. While some charts are printed in black and white, the charts in this book are all printed in color with a different ink representing a different color of floss. Where two shades of the same color are used, the color box will also include a symbol. One square on the chart equals one complete cross stitch.

Don't be fooled by the size of the printed chart because it will not necessarily be the size of your com-pleted cross stitch—that is determined by the number of threads per inch of your fabric.

If your design is 98 stitches wide by 126 stitches high, the design will be 7" wide x 9" high when worked on 14-count aida, but almost 9" x 11 1/2" when worked on an 11-count aida.

How to Get Started

Each of the charts indicates the size of the fabric required for that design. Be sure to cut a large enough piece of fabric. The fabric should be cut along the holes of the fabric so that the cut fabric is true. If you are not working on a frame, some raveling may occur as you work on the fabric. It is wise, therefore, to pre-vent any chance of this happening right at the begin-ning by overcasting the edges with a basting thread or working a machine zigzag.

The design should be worked centered on the fabric. The arrows printed on the design indicate the centers. Follow the arrows to find the center of the design. Next, you will need to find the center of the fabric. You can either count the threads, or you can fold the fabric in half and then in half again. You might want to mark this center either with a safety pin or with a cross stitch which can be removed later. You can also place horizontal and vertical threads that will cross at the center. These threads can later be removed. If the design is very complicated, try placing a thread every 10 holes in both directions, creating a grid on the fabric. This will make counting easier.

When you start stitching, it is best to start at the top of the design, or at the top of a large color area. If you work downward, you will be bringing your needle up through an empty hole and down through a used hole. Not only is it easier to bring the needle up through an empty hole than through an already occupied hole, but it will also make your stitching look neater.

Decide with which color you are going to begin your stitching. Start with a working length of floss that will be comfortable for you, probably about 18". Separate the strands of floss and then realign them to create a smooth even surface. If you are working with several colors, you might want to prepare several threaded needles in advance.

Most of the time you will be working with two strands of floss for all cross stitches and French knots. One strand is used for backstitches and straight stitches (unless otherwise noted). If you find it difficult to thread your needle with two strands of floss, try this method: Fold the two strands over the needle, slip the needle out and then push the folded edge through the eye of the needle.

Begin your work by bringing the needle up from the back to the front of the fabric. Keep about an inch of thread against the back of the fabric; then, hold it in place with the first few stitches. Once you have started to work, you can finish threads and begin new ones by weaving threads through the backs of stitches of the same color.

The Stitches

Cross Stitch: The basic cross stitch is usually done in two motions. The thread is brought up from the underside and then down again from the topside.

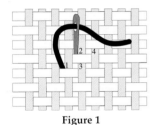

Figure 1

In **Figure 1**, the number 1 shows the needle coming up from the bottom left-hand corner of the first stitch and going down through the hole (2) at the top right-hand corner. Bringing the needle up again at number 3 and down again at number 4 will create the first half of the first two stitches.

Figure 2 shows the cross stitches being completed. Number 5 shows where the needle will come up; then needle goes down at number 6; up again at number 7 and down at number 8. You will have completed two cross stitches.

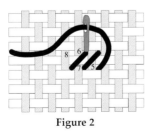

Figure 2

Wherever possible, the cross stitches should be worked in horizontal rows, completing half of each stitch across the row and then completing the stitch on the return.

Some of the designs in this book are worked over two threads. In this case, each stitch crosses diagonally over two threads in each way: up two and over two. Each square on the chart represents two warp threads and two weft threads. Count the threads, not the spaces. Imagine climbing a ladder; count the rungs, not the spaces.

While this may sound confusing, once you get started it is almost self-explanatory. You will begin to see in twos, and if you make a mistake, it will be obvious because of the slant of the stitches.

Backstitch: Backstitches are worked after the cross stitches have been worked. **Figure 3** shows the method for working backstitches: bring the thread up at odd numbers and down at even numbers.

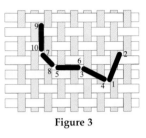

Figure 3

Straight Stitch: A straight stitch is actually a long backstitch. The needle comes up at one end and goes down at the other. The chart indicates the length and the direction of the stitch.

French Knot: The French knot used in cross stitch is made just as it is in any other form of embroidery. The floss is brought up where it is indicated on the chart. Then the floss is wrapped once around the needle and reinserted close to where it has been brought up but at least one fabric thread away. The wrapping thread is held tightly, and the needle is pulled through the wrap. The floss is released as the knot tightens. French knots can be made in the middle of a square space or at a corner between cross stitches.

Ribbon Embroidery

Several of the designs in this collection are enhanced with ribbon embroidery, a beautiful technique that uses ribbon instead of floss.

The designs here use ribbon in 2, 4 and 7-millimeter widths. The color key gives you the width and color for the required ribbon.

While there are a number of different kinds of needles that can be used for ribbon embroidery, a tapestry needle will work very well. They are good for making a big enough hole in the fabric for the ribbon to go through, and they are the needles you will have on hand for your cross stitch projects.

Cut the ribbon into short lengths, about 14". Thread one end through the eye of the needle, and pull the tail through to exceed the length of the needle. Push the needle through the tail—about $1/2$" from the end. Hold the point of the needle, and pull the long end of the ribbon to hold it on the needle. This will keep the ribbon from sliding out of the eye as you work.

Do not pull your stitches too tightly. The full width of the ribbon should be evident in all stitches. You can loosen, raise or flatten your stitch before you move on to the next stitch. Just run your needle under the stitch, moving it back and forth, until you are pleased with the results. Unlike thread, ribbon is very forgiving and easily pushed into the desired look.

Although there are many stitches that can be used for ribbon embroidery, the projects in this collection use only four stitches, straight stitch, French knot, loop stitch, and couching.

Straight Stitch: Bring the needle up from the back of the fabric at the spot indicated on the chart. Flatten the stitch, and insert the needle into the ending point indicated on the chart, gently pulling to keep the ribbon flat.

French Knot: Both single and double French knots are made in the same manner as they are made in cross stitch. They should, however, be made more loosely than when making French knots with floss. Bring the needle up where indicated on the chart; wrap the ribbon once or twice around the needle, and insert the needle into the fabric close to where it was brought up at first. Release the wrapping as the knot is formed.

Loop Stitch: The Loop Stitch is created with the help of some type of small round object, such as a pencil or a drinking straw, which can be used as a ribbon holding device. Pull the ribbon up from the back where indicated on the chart and insert the needle down part way through the fabric very close to the point of entry, making a ribbon loop. Insert the holding device through the loop, and pull the ribbon snug to hold its shape. Keep the holding device in place until you have begun working the loop for the next petal, then remove it and use it for the next loop.

Couching: Both ribbon and floss are used in couching. The ribbon is stretched flat on the fabric, and the floss is used to hold it in place. Bring the ribbon up at the spot indicated on the chart and extend it to the end. Bring the floss up and down at the spots indicated on the chart. Ribbon can also be couched with French knots.

Finishing

If the completed embroidery is soiled, wash with a gentle soap in cool water and rinse well. Roll in a towel and squeeze out excess moisture. If the embroidery has not been soiled, merely dampen it. Place the moistened embroidery face down on a dry towel. Press very carefully, being especially careful not to press down the raised stitches.

When you frame your work, be sure to mount it on an acid-free backing surface. If you like a puffy look, place some fleece beneath the embroidery.